USING RULERS AND TAPE MEASURES

Lorijo Metz

PowerKiDS press
New York

Dedicated to Suzanne, who has patience to measure

Published in 2013 by The Rosen Publishing Group, Inc.
29 East 21st Street, New York, NY 10010

First Edition

Editor: Amelie von Zumbusch
Book Design: Kate Laczynski

Photo Credits: Cover Peter Dazeley/Photographer's Choice/Getty Images; p. 4 Tetra Images/Getty Images; p. 5 KidStock/Blend Images/Getty Images; p. 6 Alex Maclean/Photonica/Getty Images; p. 7 (top) Karen Roach/Shutterstock.com; p. 7 (bottom) Jade Brookbank/Photodisc/Getty Images; pp. 8 (top), 12 (top), 21 iStockphoto/Thinkstock; p. 8 (bottom) Smile Studio/Shutterstock.com; p. 9 Denis Kuvaev/Shutterstock.com; p. 10 Yuri Arcurs/Shutterstock.com; p. 11 Wichan Kongchan/Shutterstock.com; p. 12 (bottom) Feng Yu/Shutterstock.com; p. 13 Roger Charity/StockImage/Getty Images; p. 15 Robert Crum/Shutterstock.com; p. 16 visionaryft/Shutterstock.com; p. 17 oliveromg/Shutterstock.com; p. 19 GeoAtlas map; p. 20 Ariel Skelley/Blend Images; p. 22 oksana2010/Shutterstock.com.

Library of Congress Cataloging-in-Publication Data

Metz, Lorijo.
Using rulers and tape measures / by Lorijo Metz. — 1st ed.
p. cm. — (Science tools)
Includes index.
ISBN 978-1-4488-9688-2 (library binding) — ISBN 978-1-4488-9834-3 (pbk.) —
ISBN 978-1-4488-9835-0 (6-pack)
1. Length measurement—Juvenile literature. 2. Rulers (Instruments)—Juvenile literature. 3. Tape measures—Juvenile literature. I. Title.
QC102.M48 2013
530.8—dc23

2012032008

Manufactured in the United States of America

CPSIA Compliance Information: Batch #W13PK4: For Further Information contact Rosen Publishing, New York, New York at 1-800-237-9932

CONTENTS

Measuring Distance

Distance is a measure of how far one point is from another. When someone asks how tall you are, what they want to know is the distance between the bottom of your feet and the top of your head. Rulers and tape measures are tools that people use to measure distance.

Tape measures are also known as measuring tapes.

Rulers are made out of several things, including wood, metal, and plastic.

Rulers are long, thin rectangles with marks for measuring. Most rulers do not bend. They are good for measuring straight distances. Tape measures also have marks for measuring. They are made of cloth, soft plastic, or thin metal that bends. People use tape measures to measure longer distances and curves.

Inches, Feet, and Yards

Football fields are measured in yards. The distance in yards from the nearest goal line is marked on a field.

In the United States, the units we use to measure distance come from an old system that based measurements on parts of the human body. An inch was the width of a thumb. As you might guess, a foot was the size of a foot! Today, an inch is a set distance. Twelve inches equal one foot. Three feet equal one yard.

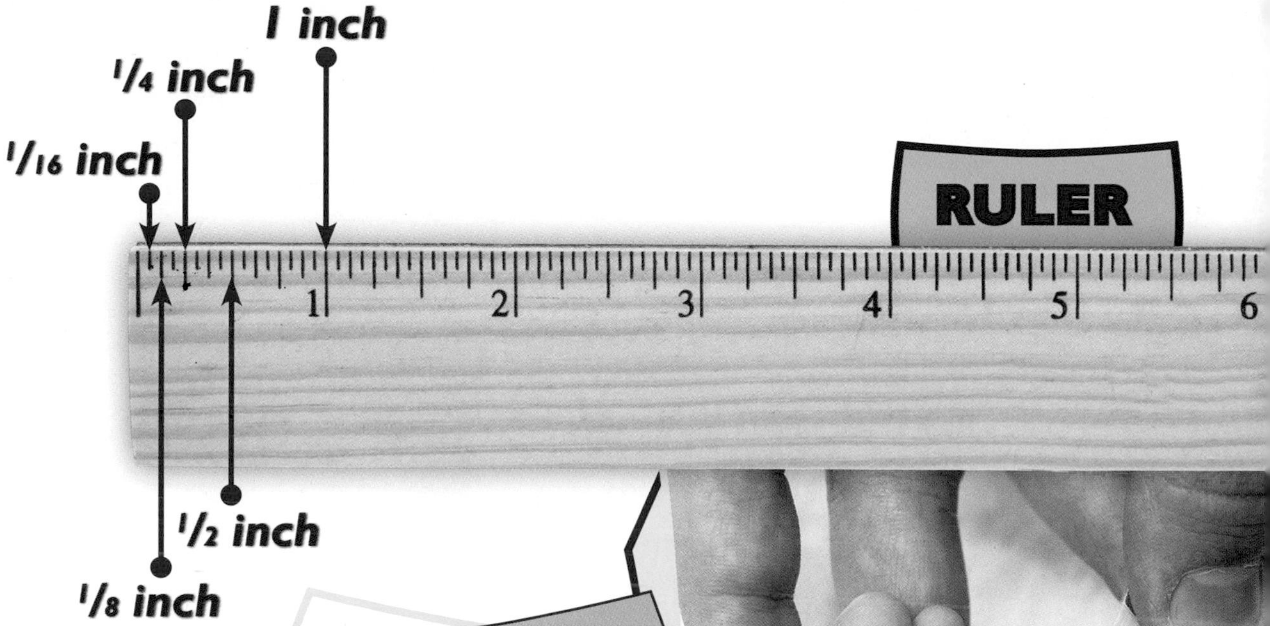

1 inch
1/4 inch
1/16 inch
RULER
1/2 inch
1/8 inch

Doctors around the world measure newborn babies. The doctors in the United States generally take their measurements in inches.

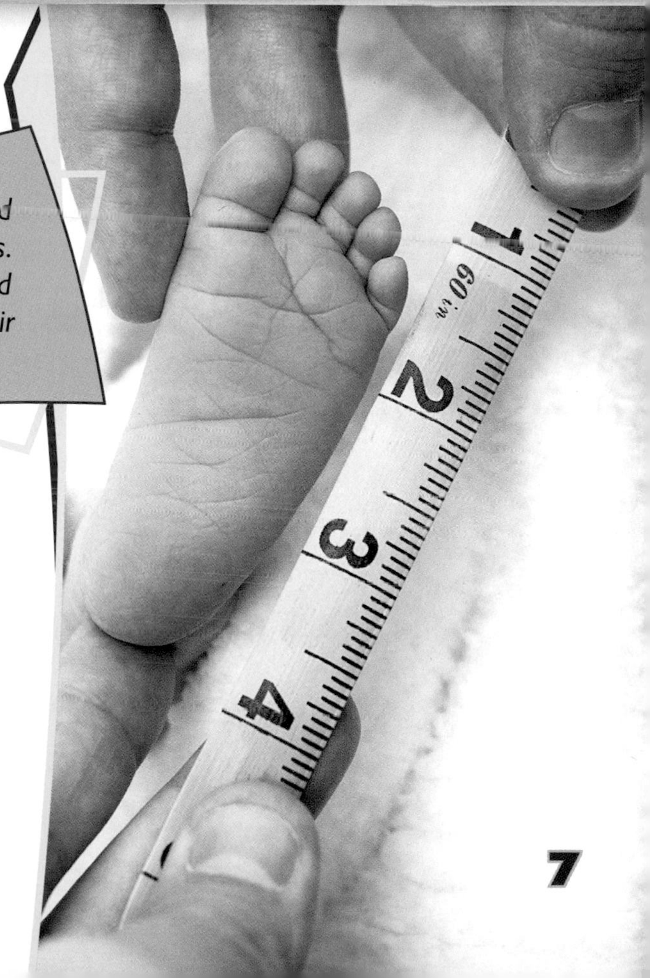

On rulers and tape measures, long, bold lines with numbers beside them measure inches. Shorter lines **divide** each inch into smaller measurements. When inches are divided into eight parts, each line equals one-eighth of an inch.

The Metric System

In 1790, scientists in France invented a system for measuring things called the **metric system**. Today, people in many countries measure distance using the metric system. Scientists use it, too. The basic unit in the metric system is the meter. The metric system is easy to use because it is a **base-ten** system, just like the number system we use.

Some rulers show both centimeters and inches. To switch the units you are measuring with, just spin the ruler in a half circle.

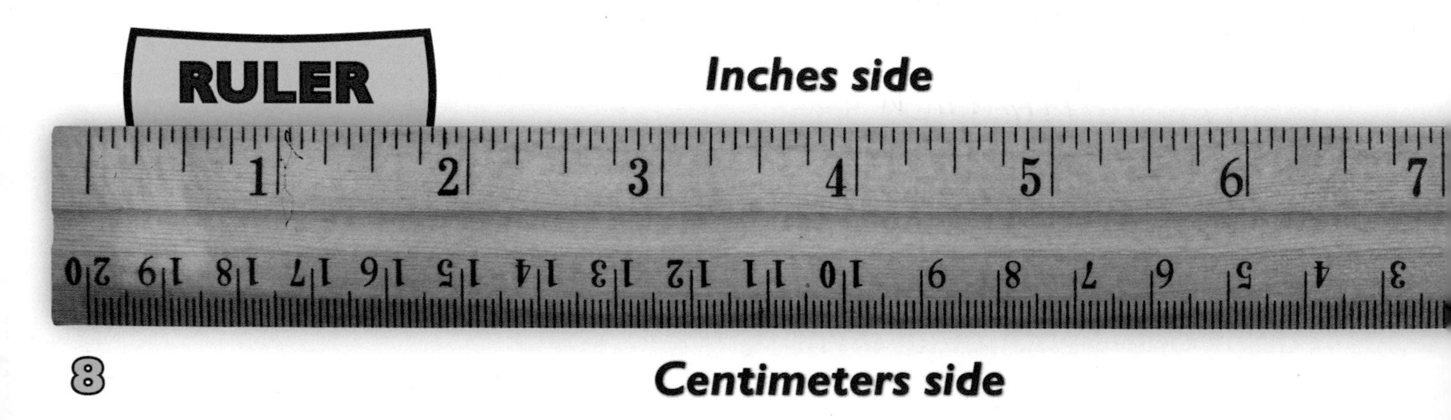

The close-together lines on metric rulers and tape measures show millimeters. The longer lines with numbers beside them measure centimeters. There are 10 millimeters in 1 centimeter and 100 centimeters in 1 meter. If you compare inches to centimeters, 1 inch equals about 2.5 centimeters.

Some races are measured in meters. One of the most famous is the 100-meter dash.

Length, Width, and Height

When you take an object's **dimensions**, you measure its width, length, and height. If you are measuring an object, such as a brick, how do you decide which side is the length, which is the width, and which is the height? There is no real right answer for this.

If you are measuring a person's height, it is easy to guess which direction to measure!

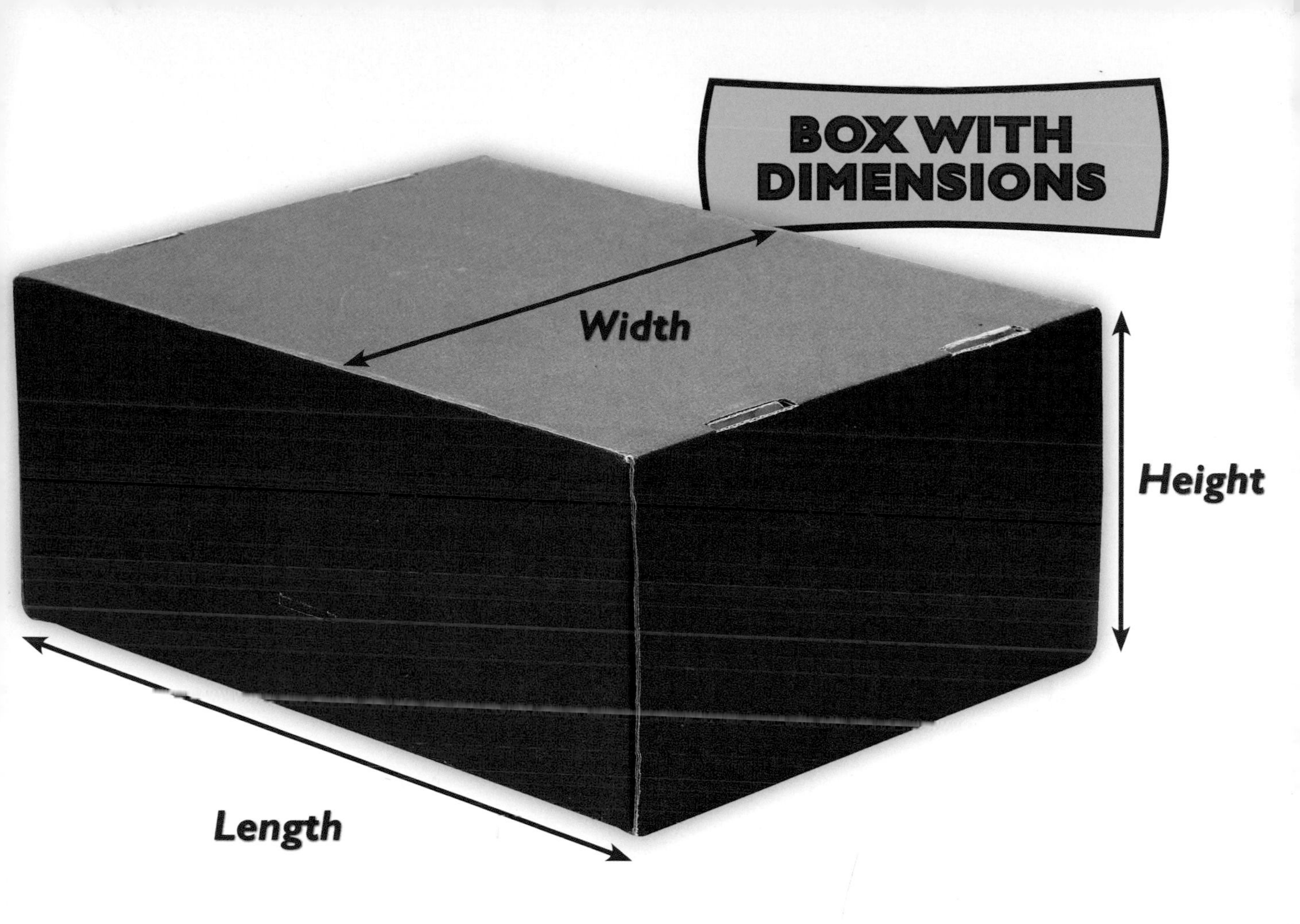

People usually call the side rising up from the ground the height. They tend to call the longest of the other sides the length and the side going off the other direction the width. If you share your measurements, explain how you decided to label each side to avoid confusing people.

Measuring Tips

To measure something, line up one end of the object you want to measure with the **zero edge** of your ruler or tape measure. The zero edge is often the straight edge to the left of the number one. Sometimes the zero edge is the first line on the ruler but is in slightly from the end.

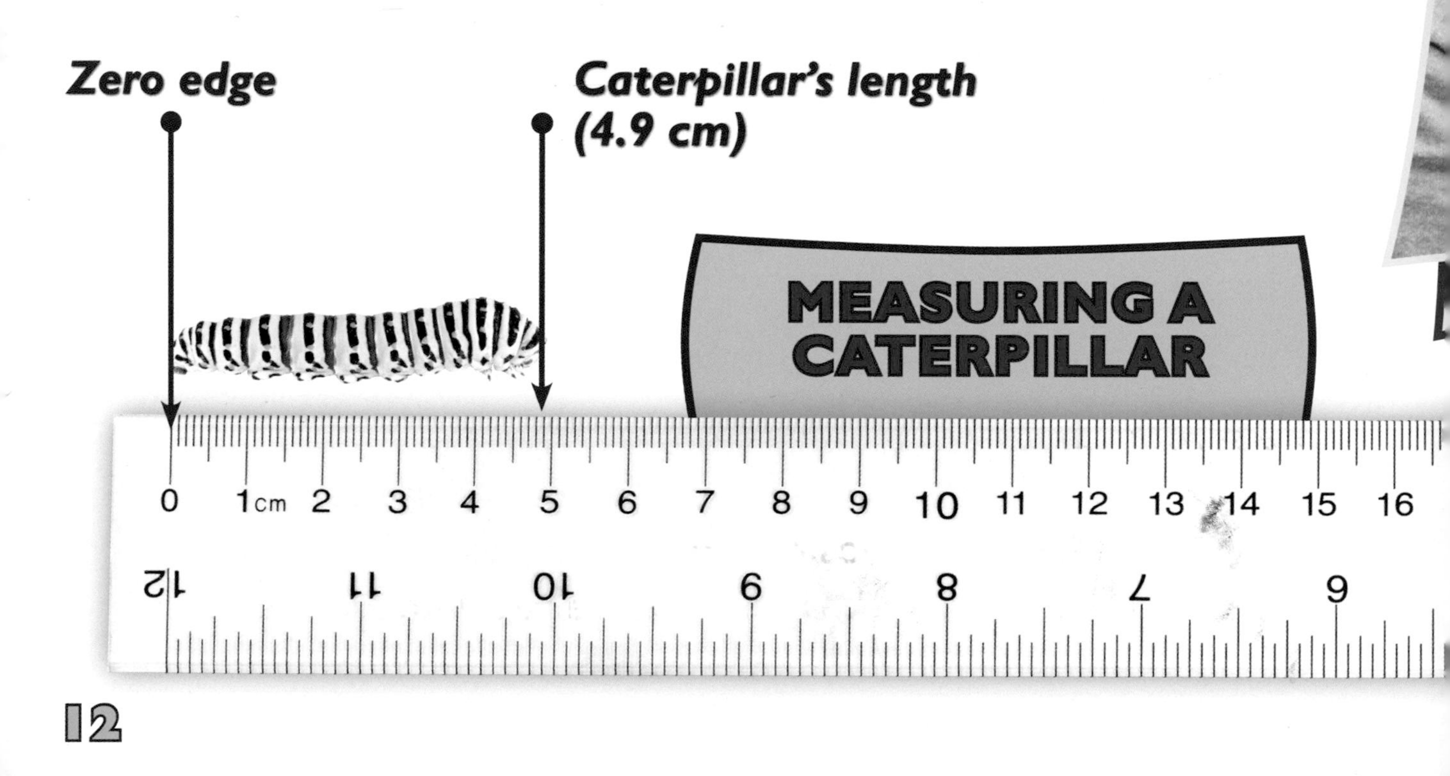

If you are measuring the width of a circle, make sure to measure at the widest point. The width of a circle is known as its diameter.

Be sure to check where it is on the ruler or tape measure you are using.

Next, look at the opposite end of your object. The mark on the ruler or tape measure that it lines up with gives you your measurement.

Planning an Experiment

Scientists notice things and question how they work. They form **hypotheses**, or ideas that try to answer these questions. To test their hypotheses, they run **experiments**.

The measurements used in experiments need to be as exact as possible. When you are measuring for an experiment, your ruler should always lay flat. Read it from above and straight on. Rulers slip easily. Make sure your ruler is lined up correctly before measuring with it. If you use a tape measure, make sure to pull it tight before reading it. A loose tape measure will give you an incorrect measurement.

This scientist is measuring a Douglas fir. When measuring the distance around a tree or other tall object, make sure to keep the tape measure the same distance above the ground.

Studying How Things Grow

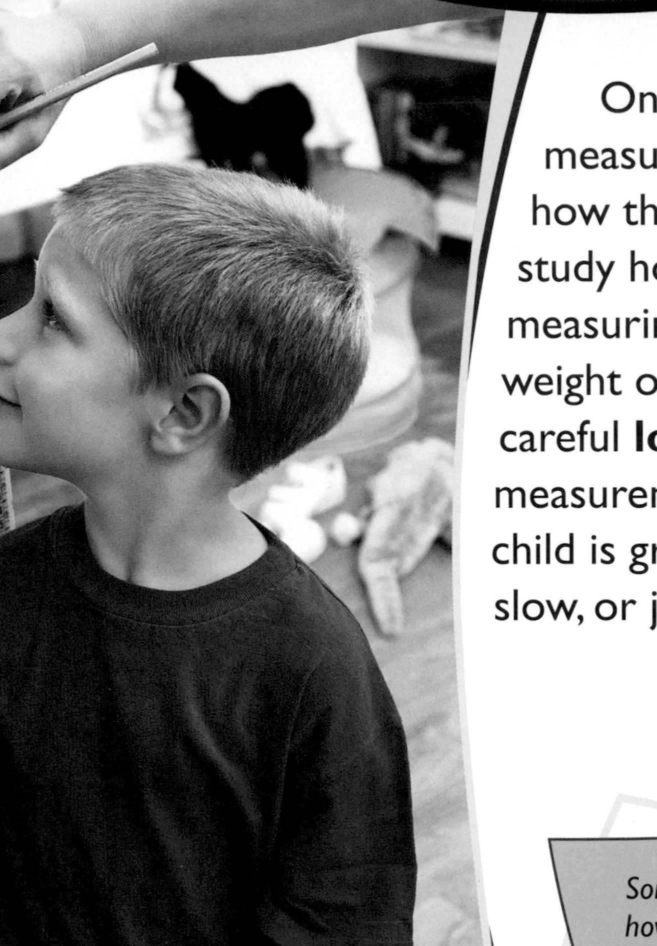

One reason that people measure things is to study how they grow. Doctors study how children grow by measuring their height and weight once a year. Keeping a careful **log**, or record, of these measurements tells them if a child is growing too fast, too slow, or just right!

Some parents keep track of how quickly their kid grows by marking the kid's height on a doorframe.

There are many experiments you can do to study how plants grow. For example, you can compare how they grow in sunlight and in the shade.

Farmers study how plants grow to learn under which **conditions** they grow best. For example, some plants grow better with a lot of water and some grow better with very little. Keeping track of how much a plant grows from day to day is one way to judge how healthy the plant is.

Measuring Distance on a Map

It's fun to plan a trip using a map. First, plan your **route**. This is the path you take to get from your starting point to the place you want to go. Many routes are not straight lines. Use a string to measure your route on a map. Then measure the string with a ruler or tape measure.

Can you use this map, a string, and a ruler to figure out how long the route from Greenville to Camden is? How does that compare to the direct distance between them?

Next, locate the **map scale**. This shows how distances on a map compare to distances in real life. For example, it may show that 1 inch (2.5 cm) on your map equals 100 miles (161 km). If your string measures 4 inches (10 cm), your route would be 400 miles (644 km) long.

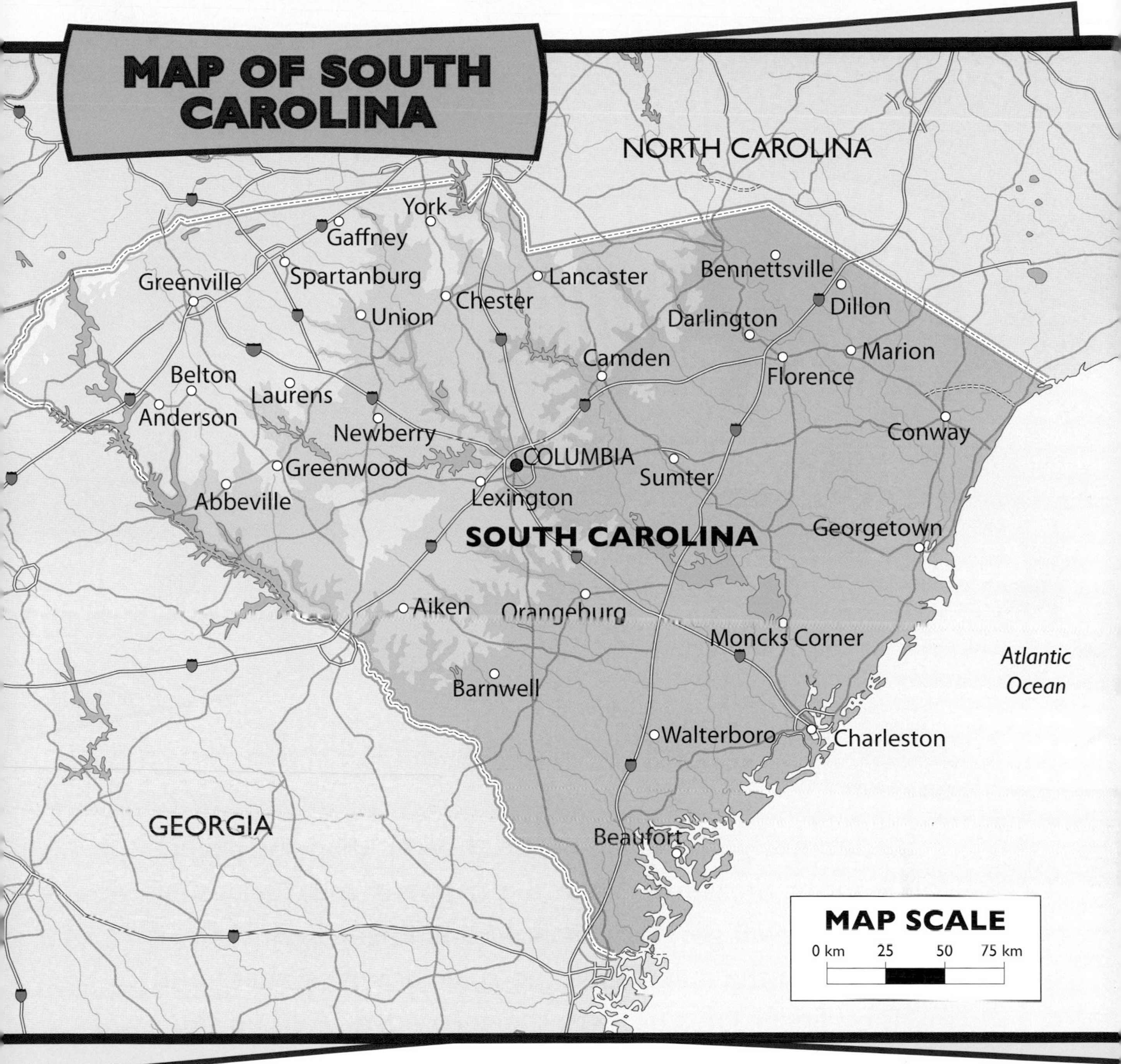
MAP OF SOUTH CAROLINA
NORTH CAROLINA
York
Gaffney
Greenville
Spartanburg
Lancaster
Bennettsville
Chester
Union
Dillon
Darlington
Marion
Camden
Florence
Belton
Laurens
Anderson
Newberry
Conway
COLUMBIA
Sumter
Greenwood
Abbeville
Lexington
SOUTH CAROLINA
Georgetown
Aiken
Orangeburg
Moncks Corner
Atlantic Ocean
Barnwell
Walterboro
Charleston
GEORGIA
Beaufort
MAP SCALE
0 km
25
50
75 km

Creative Measuring

Some things, such as stop signs, are made up of many straight edges. To figure out how long these measure around, measure each edge. Then add all the measurements together.

Sometimes your ruler may be shorter than the object you want to measure. When this happens, measure as far as the ruler will go. Mark or hold one finger against the last mark on the ruler. Slide the ruler down so that your mark or finger lines up with the zero edge. Add up the distances you measured to get the full distance.

Measuring things can be fun. Use your imagination. What if you don't have a tape measure or a ruler with you? You can measure with a string or even a blade of grass. Measure those later with a ruler or tape measure.

Finding objects to practice your measuring on can be a lot of fun. Be creative!

TIME TO MEASURE

In this experiment, you will be measuring pencils! You will need:

1. One ruler
2. Six new, sharpened pencils
3. A notebook or piece of paper to use as a log

Give a new pencil to five classmates. Keep the other new pencil for yourself. Write the names of everyone with a new pencil in your log. Measure the pencils from the tip of the eraser to the tip of the lead. Record the length of the new pencils next to each name.

Ask your classmates to use these pencils whenever they need to write. Every day for a week, measure each pencil at noon. Write these measurements in your log. At the end of the week, compare the results.

GLOSSARY

base-ten (bays-TEN) A system of numbers that uses 10 as its base.

conditions (kun-DIH-shunz) The ways people or things are or the shape they are in.

dimensions (duh-MEN-shunz) The length, width, or height of an object.

distance (DIS-tens) The length between two points.

divide (dih-VYD) To break apart or separate.

experiments (ik-SPER-uh-ments) Actions or steps taken to learn more about something.

hypotheses (hy-PAH-theh-seez) Possible answers to problems.

log (LOG) A record of day-to-day activities.

map scale (MAP SKAYL) Something that shows how the measurements on a map compare to measurements on Earth.

metric system (MEH-trik SIS-tem) A method of measurement based on counting tens.

route (ROOT) The path a person takes to get somewhere.

zero edge (ZEE-roh EDJ) The place on a ruler or tape measure from which you should start measuring.

INDEX

WEBSITES

Due to the changing nature of Internet links, PowerKids Press has developed an online list of websites related to the subject of this book. This site is updated regularly. Please use this link to access the list:
www.powerkidslinks.com/scto/ruler/